D1093918

# Body Language

## ".. the art of seeing what others are thinking"

*".... I want to congratulate you upon this piece of work .... you have a most effective book which ought to help anyone who sincerely desires to live a more creative life and achieve success along the way ...."*

*NORMAN VINCENT PEALE*
*September 24, 1979*

Distributed in Australia by:

JOSEPH BRAYSICH AUSTRALIA
Box 482, Milsons Point, Sydney, Australia 2061

BUSINESS VIDEO (NZ) LTD.
P.O. BOX 434 AUCKLAND
TELEPHONE 784-434
TELEX NZ 2838
FAX 786-550

National Library of Australia
CARD Number and ISBN 0 9595510 1 X
Published by Joseph Braysich Australia
Printed in Singapore by Tien Wah Press Pte. Ltd.

# Body Language

## A handbook by

## Joseph Braysich

*Ph.D., M.S. (Wisconsin), A.I.T. (W.A.)*
*Dip. Ed. Admin., Dip. Soc. Sc., T.C.,*
*F.A.I.M., F.I.E.A., F.I.D.A., F.A.M.I.*

Joseph
Braysich Australia

AUSTRALIA   Level 3, 98 Alfred Street, (Box 482)
Milsons Point, Sydney, Australia 2061

*Robin*

*Jeffrey, Karen, Benjamin*

# To begin ...

'What's the matter with you?'

'Nothing! ......'

Sound familiar? ... it's another instance of communication breakdown. Social scientists have verified that 70% of the message transmitted during face-to-face communication is non-verbal, that is, *BODY LANGUAGE*. In the above exchange something was the matter, unspoken maybe, but seen and felt.

Research into communication has been active since the 1950's but it is only recently that social scientists and the public, particularly the business and commercial sectors, have become excited by *BODY LANGUAGE*. One reason advanced by today's generation for this upsurge in interest is the prevailing feeling that 'You can't believe anyone anymore .....'

The topic 'Communication' is included on most companies' conference agendas; communication breakdown is the marriage counsellors' favourite subject; parents speak of the communication gap when discussing their teenaged children and company executives blame poor communication for all their problems.

This handbook sets out to cover this challenging subject from a rarely discussed viewpoint — the non-verbal aspects of face-to-face relationships or *BODY LANGUAGE*.

1

The approach is different. No lengthy, closely-set manuscript of theoretical assumptions but easy to follow illustrations, empirically tested and validated in countless reels of video and film in six countries over the past two decades.

Eminent sociologists, psychologists and linguists have added their research findings to this new approach to communication and collectively agree that it doesn't really matter what is said, if the accompanying gestures, postures and actions belie the words spoken. It has further been suggested that these subconsciously derived actions (*BODY LANGUAGE*) reflect the truth more so than the spoken word.

In the writing of this book, conceptualised during my doctoral student days at the University of Wisconsin, many video sequences were studied and analysed; vast quantities of literature researched and hundreds interviewed. Later, my own college students in Sociology classes were prevailed upon to test and verify hypotheses; even commercial companies helped by allowing me to film and research. actual showroom-floor sales sequences and boardroom interaction.

Essentially, this is a working manual for executives, sales managers, sales persons and those interested in expanding their conscious awareness of the non-verbal dimension of communication. Their reward — a better grasp of the *real message* being transmitted and received.

JOSEPH BRAYSICH
Perth, Western Australia
February, 1979

# BODY LANGUAGE

Recent advances in interpersonal relationship studies now make it possible for an individual to develop new and better methods of working with his peers. Many studies have been undertaken to examine the communications and interaction that occur between individuals in conversation.

In the last decade, research emanating from the universities of England and the United States in particular have demonstrated that the non-verbal aspects of communication play a far more important role than was previously recognised.

It has been stated, in fact, that 70% of communication exchanges are non-verbal or body language.

That is to say, the verbal component of any face-to-face conversation may account for as little as one-third of the total message. Further, research shows that the non-verbal aspect outweighs the verbal in both accuracy and validity.

Body language plays an especially important part in the lives of women. Studies have found women to be more sensitive to non-verbal cues than men. For example, each study established that women were more affected by non-verbal communication than were their male counterparts.

Other investigations undertaken in the United States proved that women were better than men at identifying various emotions portrayed non-verbally by male or female actors, and were superior to males in perceiving implications from conversation.

Victor Hugo was reported to have said that while men have foresight women have insight.

Interestingly, the studies also noted that men in the aesthetic areas of drama, art and theatre were as sensitive, if not slightly more sensitive than women to non-verbal cues in communication.

Body language and the awareness of non-verbal cues was an outgrowth of interest taken in the development and teaching of the art of negotiating, a technique of great importance in today's commercial world.

It was found, after viewing film and video-tape sequences of negotiation exchanges, that verbal communication did not operate in a vacuum, but rather that words were accompanied by a complementary process of body movements, and it is only by considering the two together that the progress of any negotiation can be determined. From these films it was also determined that subconscious and sublimated thoughts were openly expressed in body movements.

One of the earliest documented incidents involving non-verbal communication, is recorded in the story of the horse 'Clever Hans'. In the early 1900's, a gentleman in Germany, Herr Osten, trained a horse, who by tapping his hoof was able to count, add, multiply, divide, subtract and solve arithmetical problems.

Osten exhibited his horse to amazed audiences throughout Europe and with uncanny accuracy Hans did his sums.

At first, a public investigating committee failed to find any reason for Hans' apparent genius, but admitted that no trickery was involved. However, a second committee under the scientist, Pfungst, demonstrated that Hans could only answer a problem if people in his visual field knew the answer.

It was discovered that when Hans was given the question, the audience assumed an expectant posture and increased their body tension. The tension was so great as Hans neared the correct answer that the horse was able to discern this almost unconscious movement and stop tapping at the correct moment. He was responding to the non-verbal cues or body language signals of his human audiences.

It is common knowledge that people too subconsciously read body signals. They perceive others as being friendly or unfriendly, often before a word is spoken. The comment that '... the boss is a good guy once you get to know him ...' is indicative of this non-verbal perception and a sad commentary on how non-awareness of the importance of body language limits the managerial potential of an executive.

As someone gains awareness of non-verbal behaviour and attempts to interpret the body language of others, so he becomes inwardly conscious of his own body gestures. This results in more effective communication both ways.

In the study of body language it is important not to make interpretations from single unrelated gestures which could be, and often are, misleading. What must be sought is a *GESTURE CLUSTER,* that is, a set of related movements, perhaps of arms, feet, head, and inclination of the body, which together make for meaningful interpretation.

Each gesture is akin to a word in language. An isolated word is often meaningless. It is only after a series of words is placed together in a sentence that a message becomes clear. Similarly with *GESTURE CLUSTERS.*

Body gestures rely to a great degree on subconscious empathy or subconscious emotions, while the spoken word follows carefully planned thought. This is why body language often belies the spoken word and communication researchers hold that probability favours the non-verbal gesture cluster to be the more accurate when correctly interpreted.

Body language can be used as a checking device to discover whether an individual's non-verbal message matches what he is saying. In this way, a negotiating party can determine what his opposite number is really thinking. He could be saying 'No' and gesturing 'Maybe'.

Body language is a way to 'see' what others are thinking. Many body movements people make reveal attitudes and state of mind. Facial expression, eyes and deportment reveal their subconscious thoughts far more accurately than cautiously chosen words.

Everyone speaks *BODY LANGUAGE*, but its interpretation and understanding is open only to those people who take the time to learn the 'language'.

The study of body language, known also as *kinesics*, is one of the newer behavioural science techniques.

Being aware of *BODY LANGUAGE* and observing it in action is fairly simple. Interpretation is somewhat more complex and takes careful study and analysis to gain accuracy.

To better understand *BODY LANGUAGE,* adopt the following procedures:

1. Keep an open mind.
2. Observe your own posture and gestures when you are in differing moods and frames of mind. Ask yourself these questions:

   What is my body language saying? Where are my hands? Am I leaning forward or back? Are my legs crossed? Is my chin up? Is my head to the side? Are my hands clenched? What am I feeling?
3. Observe the body language of others. Initially just note that the other person is constantly moving. These movements indicate thought and emotion. As you develop a dictionary of body language signals, you will learn to read their meaning.
4. Learn to put the message you are receiving from the signals together with the spoken message and draw conclusions.
5. Learn to control your own body language so as to emit only those signals you want to send.

Finally, treat *BODY LANGUAGE* as a new language which though foreign to begin with, can be mastered with practice. Follow a study of this book with observations of *BODY LANGUAGE* encounters at the office, social gatherings and at home. Television interview programs also provide a ready source for study.

If the technique is to be used seriously in business, engage in video-tape analyses of negotiations, management discussions, sales presentations and the like with a trained observer who can point to the non-verbal cues as they occur. After a very short time it will be found that you can become proficient

in

## *BODY LANGUAGE*
*the art of seeing what others are thinking*

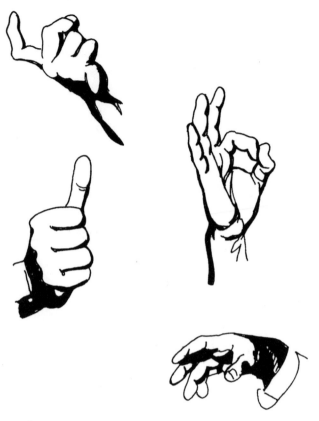

Fig. 1    Common hand gestures. 'Come here', 'O.K.', 'Ta-ta
Goodbye'.

Body gestures are common to all societies. **Illustration 1**,
shows the commonly recognised hand signals for 'Come
here', 'O.K.', the child's 'Ta-ta or good-bye'.

These gestures along with many others are learned behaviour
patterns children develop at school. The gestures are nation-
ally or culturally determined and may not bear any signifi-
cance when displayed outside the country of origin.

Body language gestures differ between cultures. The most common example of this would be the use of the thumb as "one" in the counting sequence of European people. **Illustration 2**, demonstrates how the European, when counting, commences with the thumb and on the count of 'two' proceeds to the forefinger. This is in direct opposition to his Australian, American and English counterparts who commence counting with the forefinger or index finger on the count of 'one', and proceed to the middle finger on the count of 'two'.

When asked why those particular fingers are chosen to indicate 'two', each group will invariably reply that it is easier. This is a simple demonstration of a learned behaviour pattern differing between cultures.

Western

European

Fig. 2    Signs are culturally determined. The Western and European methods of indicating "two".

People all over the world smile when they are happy and scowl when they are angry or sad. However, other gestures such as sticking out the tongue for instance, is a child's rudeness in Western countries while in South China a flick of the tongue indicates embarrassment.

9

A similar phenomenon occurs with the smoking habit of individuals around the world. It is common in Western culture to observe an individual smoking a cigarette between the index and middle finger as shown in **Illustration 3**. However, this is not the norm, nor is it common. In other countries of the world, particularly in Eastern Europe, a cigarette is generally smoked using the thumb and forefinger, or the thumb and fingers of the hand shown.

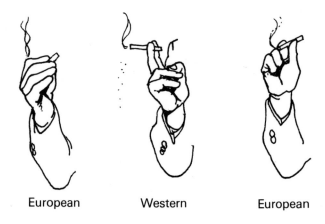

| European | Western | European |

Fig. 3    Western and European methods of smoking.

When seated the American and Australian male crosses his legs in what is known as the 'figure 4', with the ankle portion resting on the knee of the other leg, while the European male crosses the upper thighs and holds the legs more parallel.

The wearing of 'typed' clothing is also culturally determined. The well-known image of the Englishmen abroad wearing long socks and sandals is a source of amusement to his Australian and American counterparts. However, the Australian in America with his short shorts, long socks, shirt and tie is an object of curiosity, while the American wearing long shorts and tennis shoes without socks never fails to raise an eyebrow outside of the United States.

It was reported during the war that many non-verbal cues let slip by escaped Allied military personnel in Europe revealed their true identity. Examples are shown above. Can you think of more?

Boys' method of catching a ball.

Fig. 4    Some non-verbal gestures are determined by sex.

A boy adopts a different position to a girl when catching an object while seated. **Illustration 4**, shows the male with ankles touching and knees closer together than his female counterpart who utilises her skirt to help catch an object.

In communities where dresses rather than slacks or jeans were commonly worn by the girls, even the wearing of shorts during sporting fixtures did not alter this feminine tendency. However, since the advent of unisex jeans for both male and female, this sexually determined behaviour pattern is fast disappearing.

Girls' method of catching a ball.

A classical incident which demonstrates this gesture —
Huckleberry Finn, who, when disguised as a girl, was discovered because he closed his knees to catch a ball rather
than spread his lap as girls in that day and age were apt to do.
Birdwhistell, a pioneer in the field of body language, con-
cluded that most communication between people is carried
out at a subconscious level, and words which stem from the
conscious are only indirectly relevant. He estimated that
some two-thirds of the social meaning of any conversation is
body language.

A.  Obvious.                    B.  Pretend yawn.

Fig. 5      Consciousness of time.

**Illustration 5**, depicts four different body gestures, all of which show a subconscious preoccupation with 'Time'. Imagine the setting at a conference or meeting:

The first gentleman (**A**) is unsophisticated and shows an obvious approach by blatantly checking his watch. He disregards or is unaware of the feelings of others. No human relation skills.

The second (**B**) is attempting to disguise his anxiety by a forced yawn and a sneak look. One word — amateurish.

The next, surreptitiously glances at his neighbour's watch (**C**) and assumes that no one notices. Sneaky.

The last man (**D**) does not wish to offend by openly or indirectly checking his watch. Nevertheless, his subconscious preoccupation with time erupts into body language and he fiddles with his watch or watch band. This, to a trained observer, 'gives him away'. He is unaware that others can see what he is thinking.

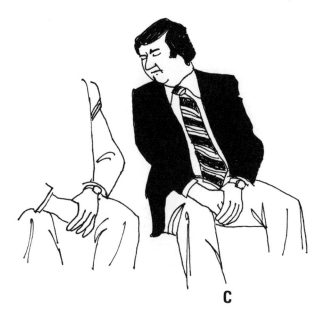

C. Sneak look.

D. Inhibited and sub-conscious touching of the watch.

Fig. 6     Telephoning who?

         A.   Addressing the manager.

B. Talking with wife or acquaintance.
C. Courting or private conversation.

**Illustration 6**, indicates the three basic telephoning positions people adopt when speaking.

To the untrained observer, someone on the telephone suggests only that he is "telephoning" — no more! The keen observer of body language however, can easily deduce the caller's identity inside three classifications.

In the first stance (**A**) the telephone is held in a manner simulating attention. The coat is done-up (defensive), the position of the body upright, so is the head (anxious), while the free hand is at clenched attention (uptight). These gestures indicate that the individual is phoning a superior or a buyer. He is addressing the telephone as if he were in the presence of that person. The caller is anxious, nervous and possibly intimidated.

In figure (**B**) there is a more relaxed manner in the body position. The head is inclined to the side, this indicates greater interest. The coat is unbuttoned, the free hand is unclasped (openness), there is a leaning back against the desk (territorial ownership) and the legs are crossed in a relaxed manner.

From the body position it could be assumed that the conversation is directed at a person with whom the caller is very much at ease, perhaps a friend, staff member, or even wife. The caller is confident, dominant and at ease.

Position (**C**) is the typical stance of an individual trying to gain the utmost privacy. The head is down, the shoulders are turned towards the wall (closed) and the voice is low (intimate). The free hand is caressing some object (courting gesture). This person is engaged in a private negotiation which he does not wish to be made public. He is attempting to shut himself off from the rest of the office.

Fig. 7     Male preening. Tucking shirt in trousers, toning sto-
           mach muscles, straightening tie.

The preening or courting gestures of both male and female in
Western cultures — **Illustrations 7 and 8**, are pronounced
and obvious. These gestures are common at a party or social
situation.

The male, **Illustration 7**, on being physically attracted to a
female is easily recognised across a dance floor or social
gathering well before he makes a move. He will commence
preening by straightening his tie and tucking in his shirt. This
is followed by the pulling in of the stomach muscles and a
more erect posture; the smoothing of the hair and buttoning
of the coat all of which forewarn females in a rather obvious
fashion.

Fig. 8     Female preening.     A.   Stroking hair.
          B.   Straightening clothes.     C.   Sitting at ease.

The female, **Illustration 8**, is also subject to preening, flirting and at-ease gestures. These are recognised by the straightening or touching of the hair accompanied by head-tossing (**A**) rearranging of clothing (**B**) sitting with one leg tucked underneath the body (**C**) crossing of the legs and sometimes balancing a shoe on the toe of one foot (**A**).

These gestures may also be accompanied by the caressing of the thigh or upper arm slowly with the fingers, or the fondling of an object. All the while the eyes are looking intensely and with interest — dilated and bright.

If the male is in close proximity the preening invariably extends to a tilt of the head, long glances, the touching of the lips with the tongue and sometimes a show of thigh, or when standing, hands on hips.

Mutual interest sparks familiarity gestures. The female may brush her partner's coat, straighten his collar or pick off pieces of cotton. All of this is done with the palm of the hand and wrist exposed toward her partner.

C

Fig. 9    Male dominance. Thumbs in belt, fingers downward.

The sexually agressive and dominant male is readily recognised by his stance — thumbs tucked into the belt with fingers
extended and pointing downwards. **Illustration 9**.

Eye contact is an important aspect of body language. For instance, people tend to look more while listening than they do when talking. Pupils enlarge at the sight of something pleasurable and contract at the distasteful or unpleasant.

If an individual, while speaking, looks at the other person for less than one-third of the time he is probably being evasive; on the other hand if he looks at the other person for more than two-thirds of the time, he is possibly more interested in that individual than in the conversation. One can conclude then, that people conversing in normal situations would tend to look at one another for roughly half to two-thirds of the time.

Dr Eckhard Hess of the University of Chicago in making detailed studies of pupil dilation discovered that even with constant light intensity, he was able to cause the pupils to dilate and contract.

His experiments demonstrated that when interest is shown in a viewed object of a pleasant nature, the pupils become activated and enlarged. On the other hand, an unpleasant sight contracts the pupils. Conclusion — pupil responses show how individuals really feel about the object, person, or situation being viewed.

In another experiment, photographs of two attractive girls were shown to a group of students. One girl had eye-drops to dilate her pupils, the other did not. Result — three times as many men selected the girl with the dilated pupils, as being more feminine and more attractive. Similar experiments at the University of Missouri with the male/female roles reversed produced much the same results.

Fig. 10    A.    Acceptance.

**Illustration 10** shows that in addition to a positive eye movement, when the object being viewed is interesting and pleasurable, the head is held up, the mouth is open and even a voiced 'Wow!' may be heard.

B.   Non-acceptance or aversion.

Conversely, disinterest and displeasure in a particular subject cause the eyes to squint, the head to turn down and pull away, the face to grimace, the teeth clamp together and a verbal 'Ugh!' may result.

According to a recent research publication from the United States the findings of Dr Hess have been applied commercially. The bulletin stated that a large firm of psychologists was testing advertising programs for companies before they committed large sums of money to any particular campaign.

The method adopted was to pick market positioning of the product, isolate its audience and then to expose a cross-section of the public to 'test' advertisements. By using sophisticated technology to measure dilation of the pupils, the amount of interest and/or disinterest registered was scientifically gauged and recorded. This, the psychologists said, indicated likely public reaction to any given advertisement.

However, while data on the nuances of pupil movement is not conclusive, researchers have yet to take body language into account (see **Illustration 10**). A study of movements of arms, hands and body would doubtless evince positive correlations and facts.

Other findings on eye contact include those of the old Chinese jade merchants who studied buyers' eyes in order to detect likes and dislikes. Card sharps too give themselves away with their eyes. A 'poker face' can't dim the light of a good hand!

Fig. 11    Stifling a comment.

Both hands over the mouth usually indicate the stifling of verbal comment. One hand over the mouth accompanied by a facial grimace similarly indicates a stifling of verbal comment. 'Oh no' could very well be the caption of **Illustration 11.**

A

B

Fig. 12    A.    Interest.    B.    Disinterest.

The gestures of the head and hands in **Illustration 12** indicate Interest and Disinterest. It is an observable phenomenon. When an individual is showing interest or enthusiasm, **figure A**, the palms of the hands will tend to be visible and the gesticulations will be in an upward motion and direction. This motion of the hands is accompanied by an ascending voice inflection and an upward tilt of the head.

The opposite of this is an indication of disinterest, **figure B** — when the head is tilted downwards, the inflection of the voice is downwards, the pointing or gesticulating of the hands is down and so with the palms.

Recapping: with interest — head up, voice up, palm up, pointing up; with disinterest — head down, voice down, palm down, pointing down.

Similarly, when asking a question the communicator is more likely to gesticulate upward and raise his voice. But when making a negative statement, such as 'No thank you', his voice tends to have a downward inflection, as do his hands.

Does your body language convey interest?

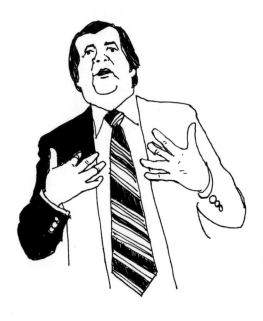

Fig. 13    Sincerity. "I give you a personal guarantee ..."

A double reinforcement of sincerity occurs if the gesture shown in **Illustration 13** accompanies conversation. The person who attempts to convey this double message of honesty does so by pointing both hands inwardly towards his chest. A variation of this pose is to have one hand over the heart and the other palm upward.

Sincerity is also displayed by moving closer, dropping the voice and touching the other person.

Fig. 14    Feet as indicators of what the mind wants to do.

The termination (mentally) of a conversation by one party or the other is often signalled by a turning of the feet and then the shoulders. **Illustration 14**.

It has been observed that feet tend to give more indication of where the mind is than does the voice. In the first illustration, the pivoted feet indicate their owner's intention to move towards the door with the body seemingly continuing the conversation. The second figure shows the turned shoulders, leaving only the head to suggest (non-verbally) that the individual wishes to remain in conversation.

Another emotion exposed by feet is that of anxiety. Feet tend to shuffle and become restless in a situation of stress. Many college professors have noticed that under stress during examinations there is a definite correlation between the amount of foot shuffling and the success of that particular candidate. Foot movement is invariably accompanied by changes in sitting posture.

Candidates in an examination who are happy with the examination paper adopt a sitting posture which does not alter frequently. However candidates who find the paper difficult are under stress and display a general restlessness of the body.

Fig. 15    Thinking about the proposition. Chin stroking.

Chin stroking, **Illustration 15**, is one of the more common and more easily recognised body language gestures. It indicates thought. People engaged in a game of chess will invariably adopt such a gesture. Notice that when the chin stroking stops the individual will tend to put the hand down, lean forward and make his move.

It is important then, not only to notice the stroking of the chin but also at what point the stroking ceases and the other actions commence.

This may be likened to a businessman who leisurely smokes a cigarette while thinking, but once the decision is made, he will tend to lean forward, butt out the cigarette and make a move.

34

Merlyn Cundiff reinforces this in her book in which she states that a prospect having made up his mind to buy, takes a deep breath and releases a big sigh. She notes that this is a sigh of relief and a sure non-verbal signal that indecision is over and the prospect is ready to take action.

Fig. 16    Critical Evaluation. Finger pointing upwards.

**Illustration 16** is a follow-on of the previous one on chin stroking except that the index finger of the hand tends to point upwards to the cheekbone. The middle finger invariably touches the upper lip while the head is somewhat more inclined. This gesture or position is one of critical evaluation and has been written up as the 'John F. Kennedy' pose.

It must be noted that when this gesture is accompanied by backward leaning or sitting right back with feet fully extended and ankles locked, the subject is deep in subconscious thought expressing doubt, cynicism and/or scepticism.

Fig. 17     Boredom.

Dejection and boredom in individuals, **Illustration 17**, is a readily perceived gesture. Usually, the subject grasps his head with both hands, with the chin resting in his palms. This is followed by a downward tilt of the head and with the face reflecting disinterest.

When one hand only is used, (see **Illustration 26**) the head is placed entirely in the palm of the hand with the chin to one side. There is no mistaking this posture of boredom.

Fig. 18    Anxiety. Hand wringing.

**Illustration 18**. Hand wringing is an indication of anxiety. The individual with a clenched fist is an up-tight person or someone who senses that he is under close scrutiny. For example, a subordinate reporting to his manager after making a wrong decision.

Fig. 19    Self Control.

**Illustration 19**. The gestures of an upright, immobile stance, the buttoned coat and the hands held together in front are all attempts at self control. The position highlights a defensive mechanism leading to withdrawal known as a 'non-person' state. This is most commonly seen in subways, at funerals, in crowded elevators, on buses and in trains.

The 'non-person' reacts as an inanimate object — he tends to avoid eye contact, does not move when touched, does not complain if his personal space is invaded and in fact is very ill-at-ease and wishes he were somewhere else.

In extreme circumstances such as in a crowded bus this body language gesture is characterised by immobility and a blank stare into space, or in an elevator at the floor numbers as they light up.

All this leads to bad communication and a non-person stance must be avoided especially when addressing a group!

Fig. 20     Defensive, uncooperative.

**Illustration 20**. The defensive uncooperative gesture. This is one which executives and managers find frightening in an audience when they are about to commence a meeting.

It depicts a defensive individual — someone with tightly folded arms high up on his chest; leaning backwards in his chair; fisted hand under the arm, head down, locked ankles with knees together and to cap it all off, a scowl.

When this gesture is marked by a leaning forward, rather than backward, it is likely that a strong resentment and even belligerence exists, particularly if the mouth is tightly closed.

Note that this pose is not to be confused with the 'evaluative' one in which the individual also folds his arms, but not as tightly or as high on the chest; the head is up and possibly inclined rather than down; the hands are not made into fists and the ankles and knees are not locked (see **Illustration 59** for a more detailed analysis).

**A**

Fig. 21    Basic head gestures.    A.    Down, defensive.

**Illustration 21**. The head is the basic indicator of a person's attitude. The head when down on the chest is a sign of defensiveness (**A**). This may be accompanied by the eyes looking down at the floor or, as the person starts to show interest, the eyes peering upwards from a downward tilted head.

The next move in the sequence (**B**) is when the head comes up. Interest is beginning to take shape in the subject's mind. He is becoming receptive.

The final drawing (**C**) shows an inclined head. This telegraphs interest. In any sales situation, whether it be the sale of a commodity or a negotiation, the inclined head is the best method of recognising willingness and cooperation. The head usually moves first.

42

B.   Up, open.     C.   Inclined, interested.

**A**

Fig. 22    Apprehension. An attempt at self control.

**Illustration 22.** Similar to **Illustration 19**, where an individual, somewhat tense and apprehensive, attempts self control. If in a seated position, he will display the body language cluster drawn in **Illustration 22**.

B

His mental condition is typified by clenched fists and locked ankles. If in a seated position with arm supports, the hands will tightly grip the chair's armrests.

This subject is up-tight with a nervous demeanor and is trying to hold back his feelings.

This body gesture is often seen in medical or dental surgeries and in speeding cars or planes where fright takes over. The buttoning of the coat is a further attempt at warding off outside influences and at withdrawal.

Fig. 23    Attentive but not convinced.

**Illustrations 23 and 24** show a reserved and unconvinced attitude. Both point to the fact that the individual is still mentally opposed to concluding a sale or settling a difference of opinion.

When one is faced with clients occupying either of these positions it is best to give more information and await a move from either the 'figure 4' (of doubt) or the extended legs with crossed ankles (a closed mind). Proceed with the negotiations when an open attitude is adopted (**Illustration 25**).

Fig. 24     "Figure 4". Has reservations, requires information and/or clarification.

Fig. 25     Open. Willing participant.

Openness or a willingness to participate is shown in **Illustration 25**. The body language includes leaning forward; sitting towards the front edge of the chair; feet flat on the floor; knees apart; hands upturned and apart and head raised. This person is willing, enthusiastic and open-minded.

Frequent shoulder shrugging and head nodding are other good indicators of agreement and cooperation.

Two things bear repeating:

1. An individual may learn to read and interpret the body signals of others but equally important is the ability to recognize and use one's own body language to advantage. In order to obtain a positive response you must send out the right body vibes yourself.

2. When studying body language it is essential to note changes in body arrangement — sitting or standing. A change in physical position usually indicates a change in mental position as well. For example, a move to leaning forward and the open stance (**Illustration 25**) indicates a positive, favourable change; whereas a sudden leaning back, a touch to the nose and folding of the arms signify a negative shift.

Fig. 26    Dissatisfied, dejected.

Dejection or boredom (**Illustration 26**) is often depicted by an individual with one hand supporting the head, and eyes half closed. He is dissatisfied with the proceedings if not totally frustrated, bored and dejected.

A variation of this may be seen in a student who doodles all over his file; or the bored executive (or salesman) who covers his blotter and papers with drawings and abstract doodles.

Fig. 27    Interrupt gesture. Fingers to mouth.

**Illustration 27**. Interrupt gesture. A subconscious wish to interrupt a conversation is usually indicated by a fleeting raising of the fingers to the mouth. Speakers recognise this gesture as 'slow down, you're going too fast'. It could also signal the posing of a question.

Salesmen would do well to watch their customers for such a sign and slow down their presentation. This signal can also be interpreted as 'Wait a minute I'd like to say something ...'.

**Illustrations 28, 29 and 30.** Negative evaluation. Each of these three illustrations show doubt, rejection and/or negation in a listener. In a speaker, they often indicate fibbing, exaggeration or downright lying.

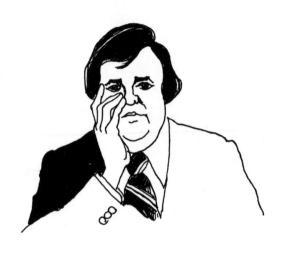

Fig. 28    Negative evaluation. Fingers to corner of eye.

Specifically, **Illustration 28**, touching the corner of the eye with the fingers (usually the middle finger) is a gesture which says: 'I can't really see it, but because you're the boss I'll go along with it ...' It is usually accompanied by a downward thrust of the head.

Fig. 29     Negative evaluation. Fingers to ear-lobe.

**Illustration 29** shows a momentary gesture with the index finger beside or behind the ear and indicates subconscious refusal to accept something which is being pointed out.

Fig. 30    Negative evaluation. Index finger under nose.

The most significant of these three negative evaluation gestures is shown in **Illustration 30** where there is a rubbing or touching of the nose with the knuckle of the index finger, or the running of the index finger horizontally under the nose. This gesture commonly denotes disbelief in the proceedings, or a speaker's exaggeration of his own claims.

Fig. 31    Exasperation, extreme frustration.

A state of extreme frustration and exasperation is often
indicated by the movement of the palm to the back of the
neck in a defensive rubbing gesture. **Illustration 31**. A
variation is the running of the fingers through the hair and
over the top of the head to the back of the neck. This hand-
to-neck action is often accompanied by a muttered 'Oh no',
'tch tch', or a hissed intake of breath through clenched teeth.

Fig. 32    Confident superiority.

**Illustration 32** shows up an unfortunate non-verbal trait of many executives and senior managers. The cluster of gestures shows hands clasped behind the head; head well back; body leaning back in a chair; legs extended; ankles invariably crossed or up on a desk. This is a position of confident superiority and general disinterest.

This individual is invariably in control and may even have a hidden advantage. The position is commonly accompanied by utterances like — 'What's the problem?' — 'You've come to the right place, I can handle this ...' .

This hands-behind-the-head position subconsciously signals to subordinates that the executive has little time for their problems. Junior staff particularly find it disconcerting and have deemed it the postural attitude most disliked in a manager.

A variation of the hands-behind-the-head pose is known as pyramiding — demonstrated in the series of **Illustrations 33A, 33B, and 33C**. Pyramiding signifies confidence.

Fig. 33     Pyramiding.     A.     Confident.

In **33A**, the fingers form a high pyramid, alluding to a smug and even egotistical frame of mind. This posture is invariably accompanied by a leaning back in the chair, feet somewhat extended, ankles crossed and head inclined downward.

**B**

B.  Reserved, confident.

**Illustration 33B**, demonstrates a less blatant show of confidence, while **Illustration 33C** in which the body inclines forward with feet apart and hands lowered, denotes a confident and interested frame of mind.

**C**

C.   Interested, confident.

Another indicator of confidence in individuals walking or standing, is shown by the hands clasped behind the back and the shoulders squared to the front. In this pose, only the head, complete with a fixed smile, turns from side to side.

Fig. 34    Confident disinterest.
Hands behind back,
head only turned.

**Illustration 34**. The first outward signs — a smile and head movement suggest interest. However, this is negated when the shoulders remain set and the hands stay clasped behind the back. Prognosis: Confident disinterest.

This posture is typical of a competent individual in authority making a routine inspection. Managers walking through an office tend to subconsciously adopt this pose, while members of English royalty are renowned for it. The cause: while the conscious mind is attempting to remain interested, the subconscious is straying, having seen it all before. Note the difference when the subject is suddenly confronted with an unexpected event — the shoulders turn, the hands unclasp and the body leans forward. All of which demonstrates a renewed interest.

61

Fig. 35    Leaning against an object. Territorial ownership. "I belong here .."

**Illustration 35.** Territorial ownership is often shown by an individual subconsciously leaning against a possession, be it his car, furniture in his new office, or home, thereby exhibiting confidence and ownership. Another common sight in a family album is a girl leaning against her boyfriend in much the same way — territorial ownership?

Fig. 36    Quiet defensiveness.

**Illustration 36** presents a somewhat nervous or defensive picture. The buttoned coat, the clenched hand and leg crossed at the ankle, all suggest an uneasy air. This stance is often seen in newcomers to a social gathering.

Fig. 37    Insecure and defensive salesman.

**Illustration 37** depicts some of the gestures likely to be adopted by the insecure and defensive salesman. Points to note are: dark sunglasses; buttoned coat; hands together; presentation folder used as a shield; and an arm crossing the chest.

Fig. 38    Confident, open approach.

In contrast, the interviewer with confidence or an under-standing of non-verbal gestures, (**Illustration 38**) unbuttons the coat, takes off the sunglasses, puts down the presentation folder and unclenches his hand. This stance is open, friendly and secure.

**IMAGE.** In addition to non-verbal gestures, acceptance is very much dependent on image, built by clothing, grooming, speech, presentation kit and even vehicle.

Image is shaped by what a person wishes to project. There is evidence to suggest that dark clothing supports a business or formal approach whereas lighter colours indicate a more casual image.

The type of pen used is significant. A chewed plastic biro conjures up a very different image from that of a modern gold or silver pen. Again, a neatly kept presentation folder is more impressive than a cheap notebook and loose papers.

Personal grooming is a non-verbal cue in itself and many a decision has been made on first impressions.

An experiment conducted with college students in Australia clearly showed that students have a fixed *modal* stereotyped image of each of the professions. An architect, for instance, is deemed modern and trendy, wearing a somewhat longer hairstyle and sporty but fashionable clothing. His hair is seen as invariably light in colour; his sporty, European car is yellow, red or white; his home a Hills area showplace and his office a functional near-city hideaway.

Findings such as this serve to remind people in business that public expectations do exist. So, people wanting to increase their market penetration should undertake market research on the image expectations for their particular trade or profession.

Fig. 39     Confident, open, aggressive approach.

**Illustration 39** again depicts the confident, open salesman now in a more aggressive mood. By leaning forward and extending an arm in a handshake he encroaches on the personal space of his client, causing him to involuntarily accept the overture or retreat. If the meeting occurs at a doorway to an office or home, the interviewer, with a wiping action of the feet, completes the non-verbal cues of seeking entry and reinforces it with 'May I come in for a moment?' He is usually asked inside.

Many an unsuspecting homeowner is at a loss to explain why some vendors are allowed access to his home while others are refused admittance. The answer lies chiefly in the body language encounter.

Fig. 40    Creating a psychological advantage.

**HANDSHAKING. Illustration 40.** It is possible to create a psychological mental distance by being first in offering a hand. Normally hands are extended simultaneously, but where one is insecure and reticent, the other can gain an advantage by being assertive. Conversely, refusing or ignoring a handshake also establishes a psychological advantage.

Close to the handshake in advantage-taking is one-upmanship in starting conversation; leading from topic to topic; and moving into the other person's *social bubble space*. These and the various handshake types will be treated at greater length in the second of this series — *Body Language in Business.*

**POWER.** Power is the ability to influence others to do as you wish, in spite of themselves. Power is not necessarily vested in authority.

It is well known that while two or more sales managers have the same authority in an organisation, their power is unequal.

Fig. 41    Demonstrating power or superiority by 'first through the door' mechanism.

**Illustration 41.** One exercise in checking power is to note who, of the two apparent equals, move through a doorway first. When two males come up to a door at the same time, one will usually go ahead of the other as if propelled by a magic formula. This is because the dominant person senses his position and goes first, while his subordinate falls back for a like reason.

When it comes to a male/female situation the older male will always give way to the female. In today's unisex business world however, the younger male is apt to move ahead of his female colleague through the office doorway, saving his gallantry for social occasions.

The male/female juxtaposition in doorways is further complicated when a male in an office is attracted to a female subordinate. He may then demonstrate a mixed-power attitude where he recognises his right to enter first, but in order to impress the girl, allows her to precede him. He maintains his power status inasmuch as he cedes from choice. She, in turn, knowingly gains a certain power in her ability to influence a superior.

Fig. 42    A.    Invading another's space.
           B.    Withdrawal.

**Illustration 42** shows power in relation to an invasion of personal space. The reaction of the girl in **figure B** to a broaching of her area by her male partner's coffee mug, is to go on the defensive by moving back and withdrawing her own coffee mug. This reaction is normally subconscious as the girl feels ill-at-ease without consciously recognising the cause.

Fig. 43    A.    Intimate distance is rejected.

B.   Social distance is accepted.

**Illustration 43** depicts a similar non-verbal reaction when personal space is intruded upon. In **figure A**, the male has encroached on the personal space of the female causing her to lean backward and away with one shoulder. The female also reacts by feeling uncomfortable which caused a drop in her level of concentration. Once the male has taken measures to move back out of the female's personal bubble she regains her composure, stands upright and squares her shoulders.

Fig. 44    Desk positions in library.
A.    Join me, but keep to yourself.

**Illustration 44.** Positioning at a desk is indicative of a person's motives. If seated in a library or cafeteria at the very end of a long desk or table (**figure A**) the subject shows receptiveness to being joined by someone prepared to keep to the other end. However, someone occupying the middle of a desk with books spread around (**figure B**) is signalling a desire to be left alone. Find a seat elsewhere!

A third seating position is off-centre but not quite at the end (**figure C**). This is usually an open, non-verbal invitation for someone to sit on the opposite side.

Individuals, in earnest search of privacy, tend to sit away from the door or in the furthermost corner of the library or cafeteria. Stay clear!

B.  Keep away.

C.  Join me if you wish.

**ORIENTATION**. Orientation is to do with the axis of the shoulders when people are conversing. Generally when people are seated *opposite* one another, they are said to be competing; if at *right angles* they are cooperating and if *alongside* they are cooperating and in intimate conversation.

Seating arrangements at bus depots and airport terminals are not conducive to close or intimate conversation. This type of seating is designed to minimise the social interaction People at an airport are generally strangers and more intimate seating would encourage fraternisation which is counter-productive to a public terminal's function.

**Illustrations 45-49, A,B,C,D,E,F,G.** This series of illustrations zeros in on how someone can change a confrontation into a session of friendly counselling simply by careful deployment of a presentation kit, body language, and the studied manipulation of distance.

**A**

Fig. 45     Move from an attitude of Superiority (A), to Interest
            (B).

**Illustration 45 (Figure A).** The subject senses that the
female seated opposite is in a classic confrontation position,
and also that his confident, dominant manner (hands behind
the head) is likely to antagonise her. So he drops his arms
and leans forward. The female responds by becoming interested. He then waits until her head is inclined to the side
(**Figure B**).

Fig. 46    Right-angle sitting and back-and-forth swinging to give
an 'at ease' impression (C).

In **Illustration 46**, (**Figure C**) the executive is swinging backwards and forwards in his chair and talking over one shoulder at right-angles to his client in a bid to make her feel at ease.

Fig. 47    Manoeuvre from 'opposite' position to 'corner' position (D).

Next in **Illustration 47 (Figure D)**, the executive manoeuvres the presentation kit to a right angled corner position which is more conducive to friendliness in an interview.

Fig. 48    Manoeuvre from 'corner' (E), to close 'alongside' (F).

Now in **Illustration 48**, (**Figure E**) the interviewer moves closer to the corner by judiciously placing his demonstration material and then (**Figure F**) he moves around the table to her side.

Fig. 49    Intimate counselling (G).

However, the executive recognises that he is higher than his client and that she could feel 'stood over', so he moves level and places the material directly in front of her.

Finally, **Illustration 49** (**Figure G**), shows the interviewer and interviewee in an intimate counselling position.

Note the close proximity and level of the bodies, the centralisation of the presentation material and the removal of the arm barrier between the individuals, all of which contribute to a marked improvement in body language relations on **Illustration 48**, (**Figure F**).

This seating arrangement (**Illustration 49**), is far more likely to gain the client's confidence and firmly establish her trust in the executive.

**GLASSES**. The use of glasses, like the use of pipes and cigarettes, is a very interesting non-verbal phenomenon.

Fig. 50     Gaining time to answer, usually critically.

**Illustration 50**. The placing of spectacle frames in the mouth is a time-gaining gesture indicative of a critical nature. The next stage sees the glasses folded slowly and deliberately and placed on the desk in front. This shows that he has reached a decision and is about to make a statement.

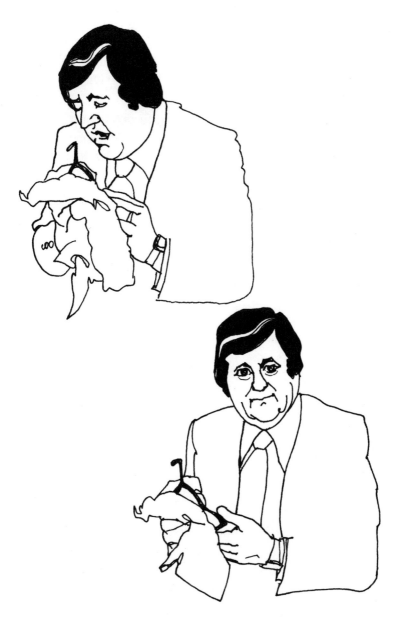

Fig. 51    Slow ritual polishing of glasses. Carefully awaiting a chance to challenge the idea, the speaker, or both.

**Illustration 51**. This slow and deliberate ritual polishing of the glasses is also symptomatic of an individual pausing for thought. He wants to stall for time in order to evaluate the situation before challenging the speaker, or at least questioning him on some aspect of his statements.

Summing up — **Illustrations 50 and 51** demonstrate a form of aggression. The person engaged in handling the glasses is exhibiting resistance to the speaker, or to his ideas, or to both.

Fig. 52     Reassurance wanted.

**Illustration 52**. The fingering of the tie, cuff-links, and ring or necklace of the female is a gesture calling for reassurance. This mental condition is similar to that of **Illustration 18** (one of anxiety) but here objects take the place of the hand.

Fig. 53     Subconscious posture of dominance.

**Illustration 53**. This person and the one in **Illustration 56** tend to be dominant personalities with leadership qualities. It is interesting to note that despite the seemingly relaxed and informal pose, and protestations of 'I feel relaxed like this', the position invariably signals a subconscious attempt to demonstrate dominance, territorial right, indifference and even hostility.

90

Fig. 54    The lint picker. Disapproves, but not prepared to 'show his hand.'

**Illustration 54.** The imaginary lint picker indicates by his actions that he disapproves of statements made in the conversation, but is constrained from saying so. He sits with legs crossed, 'Figure 4', back in his chair, flicking and picking at imaginary pieces of lint while looking down and frowning frequently.

Fig. 55     Indifference. Show territorial rights/superiority.

**Illustration 55**. Supremacy, indifference, non-concern, perhaps even hostility. The boss may adopt this posture in a subordinate's office to demonstrate superiority or just to dominate. People in their own offices adopt this stance to demonstrate territorial rights to visitors. When tackled the response is likely to be 'I'm more relaxed in this position'. The question to put then is to ask if a similar pose is taken when no one else is in the office.

However, if this posture occurs in a casual situation it may be attributed to a close friendship and disregard for common courtesies.

Fig. 56     Dominant personality. Feet on desk or drawer.

**Illustration 56.** This gentleman, like his counter-part in **Illustration 55**, is a dominant personality. He is displaying his dominance. If questioned, he too will claim that he is more 'comfortable' in that position.

Fig. 57    'I really can't see it ...'

**Illustration 57.** An individual experiencing difficulty in solving a problem, or in conceptualising a process may adopt this pose of fingers across the eyes and head down when in doubt. He really doesn't want to make a decision because he can't see the solution.

Fig. 58    'Let me see now ...'

**Illustration 58**. Pinching the bridge of the nose with the eyes closed and head downturned is a form of evaluation. This gesture indicates a deep concern or worry about the decision to be made. This individual is thinking deeply on the problem and is likely to ask for further details and clarification of doubtful issues.

**A**

Fig. 59    Posture Profile Sequence.    A.   Aggressive
B.   Defensive    C.   Interested
D.   Critical evaluation

**Illustration 59** presents a series of sitting p'ostures.

**Figure A — an aggressive, defensive posture.**
Note. Head down, arms folded tightly, fist clenched, sitting and leaning back, knees together, legs extended, ankles tightly crossed.

B

**Figure B — defensive but with some interest.**
Note. Head up, legs drawn up, knees apart — other
positions unchanged.

C

**Figure C — interest developing.**
 Note. Head to the side, fist unclenched, hand to chin, sitting more upright.

**Figure D — critical evaluation.**
Note. Finger upwards along cheekbone, head even more inclined.

When it is considered that most negotiations occur while seated, the nuances of the sitting positions should be studied carefully.

Enthusiasm, openness, and readiness are expressed in **Illustrations 60, 61 and 62**. The legs are astride, hands on hips, coat unbuttoned and swept back — a typical coach's (or sales manager's) 'achievement orientated' stance.

Fig. 60     Open readiness. Rubbing hands on thighs.

**Illustration 60**. Leaning forward, sitting on the edge of the chair, knees apart and rubbing palms on thighs is a position of open readiness. An action guaranteed to chase visitors, who have overstayed their welcome, out of your office.

Fig. 61     Achiever stance. Enthusiastic readiness.

**Illustration 61** presents the enthusiastic person who, dressed more appropriately, would pass for a runner poised on his starting blocks.

Both **Illustrations 60 and 61** show positions of a high degree of goal orientation. Each could be saying 'Well, let's get started'.

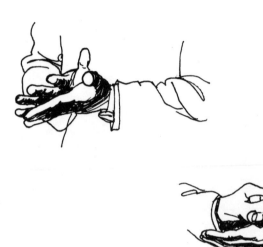

Fig. 62    Readiness gestures. Rubbing hands together, fist into palm, snapping of the fingers.

**Illustration 62** shows the rubbing of the palms, the striking of the palm with a clenched fist and the snapping of the fingers. All of these signify readiness or expectation. Usually they are accompanied by utterances like, 'Okay, let's go ...'

If in a seated position, readiness is indicated by the rubbing of the palms forward and backward on both thighs suggesting great urgency.

Fig. 63      Superior evaluative gesture.

**Illustration 63**. This gesture of peering over the top of glasses is often characterised in films on school teachers and judges. The gesture elicits a strong negative reaction from people who feel that they are being scrutinised, analysed and/or looked over. Yet many managers and executives wear half-glasses for reading without recognising the negative reaction it is likely to engender in their staff.

Fig. 64    Authoritarian, involved stance.

A dominant authoritarian stance is shown in **Illustration 64**. The gesture cluster includes — position behind the desk, an upturned finger, a leaning forward on a palm for support. All are reminiscent of the school-teacher or policeman of our childhood.

Fig. 65    Lapel holder. Smug.

Fig. 66    Waistcoat thruster. Dominant personality.

**Illustration 65 and 66**. The lapel holder and the waist coat thruster are dominant, smug, and aggressive personalities. Not common gesture clusters in today's business world.

Fig. 67     Authoritarian figure. Confident and agressive.

**Illustration 67**: Authoritarian, confident and aggressive. This stance is bolstered by the buttoned-up coat, upright posture, hands in pockets, thumbs pointing outwards. The subject may not realise that he is demonstrating his authority to the outside world but that is the message he is sending. A popular Australian business journal once ran a front cover photograph of one of Australia's millionaires in just this pose!

Fig. 68     Boss at a staff social. Extremely cautious and guarded.

**Illustration 68**. This illustration is similar to **Illustration 57** but depicts a manager at a staff social whose body language underlines his extreme cautiousness and reluctance to speak freely. (He is there to have a duty drink with the staff and no more!) This individual cannot be approached for business information as he has closed off. He emphasises this with his buttoned-up coat, thumb pointing out of the pocket, other hand occupied, with a drink. The palm tree alongside ensures privacy on one flank.

Fig. 69    Involved and interested.

Fig. 70    Involved and eager to get started.

**Illustrations 69 and 70** again show an eagerness and readiness to commence a task. The tell-tale gestures are: sitting forward on the edge of the chair, the body inclined forward, the head up, the knees apart with feet flat on the floor, the forearm across one knee while the fingers and palm of the right hand (**figure 70**) are saying 'Let's get moving'.

Fig. 71    Stages of Evaluation.    A.    Evaluation.

**Illustration 71.** The stages of evaluation are shown in the three figures. The head is seen to alter its position from upright (**A**) to inclined (**B & C**); the arm moves from across the chest (**A & B**) to on the desk (**C**); and the body moves forward (**A to C**).

These minor body movements signify a great change in attitude. To close a presentation while the individual is seated as in **Figure A** would be too early and would probably destroy the on-going negotiation. Far better to wait for the **Figure C** position and a better chance of success.

B. Head inclined but arm still shows reservation.

C. Forward in chair, arm barrier down.

Fig. 72    Seller — Buyer.

**Illustration 72. Buyer versus Seller.**

Seller:
1. Leaning forward.
2. Sitting on edge of chair.
3. Knees apart.
4. Feet flat on the floor.
5. Hands open.
6. Palms up.
7. Unbuttoned coat.
8. Smile.
9. Head up.
10. Inflection of the voice would most definitely be upward.


Buyer:
1. Leaning backward.
2. Against back of chair.
3. Knees together.
4. Feet extended and heels on the floor.
5. Hands closed.
6. Palms form pyramid.
7. Coat buttoned-up.
8. Scowl.
9. Head down, chin on chest.
10. Voice would most certainly be inflected downward.

**Illustrations 73 and 74**. This series shows a male/female interaction where the body language overtly suggests the subconscious attitude of each person towards the other. There are six basic clues to the attitude of an individual sitting in this position. They are:

1. Hands.
2. Forearm.
3. Upper leg.
4. Shoulders.
5. Body tilt.
6. Position of body.

Fig. 73    Making a new female friend.

In **Illustration 73 (Figure A)** the man has an open stance while the woman is firmly displaying a passive, non-involvement evidenced by:

1. Clenched hand.
2. The extended forearm *between* them.
3. The crossed leg *between* them.
4. The shoulders square or even worse, turned away.
5. The body tilt is away from the male.
6. The sitting position is well back.

**B**

In **figure B**, the woman is 'warming' to the overtures. This is shown by a turning of her shoulders, head, and a more forward tilt of the body.

C

In **figure C**, the woman is interested and shows it by the following:

1. The hand is held with fingers loosely apart.
2. The forearm barrier has been dropped and in fact, raised against outside interference (right hand).
3. The outside leg is now crossed over the inside leg — further evidence of interest.
4. The shoulders have turned towards the man.
5. The forward pivoting of the body continues.
6. The sitting position is forward and closer to the man.

In **Illustration 74**, the male starts off in a defensive, closed position. Can you identify the six gestures which show that he has changed from a defensive, closed position to an interested, open one?

Fig. 74    How to recognise if you are making a new male friend.

A

B

C

# To conclude ...

*BODY LANGUAGE*, you will now be aware, is as real as the English language.

You have learned that you must manage your own body movements in order to maximize your efforts. You have discovered that people often say one thing and mean another — but now you have the ability to uncover such a person.

The handbook has taught you to be on the lookout for gesture clusters and not isolated incidents which may be meaningless.

From the readings you have noted that body language stems primarily from the subconscious and therefore is a more accurate indicator of feeling than the carefully chosen word. You have been shown how you may obtain a more honest appraisal when involved in business dealings.

By using the knowledge and techniques discovered in this volume you will be better able to communicate your feelings more effectively, and if English is not your cultural tongue you have seen how necessary it is to 'catch' the body gestures in order to fully gain the meaning of an exchange.

Finally, you will be pleased that you have made the effort to learn Body Language and you will reap the rewards of these efforts. Inter-personal communication will hold no doubts for

*BODY LANGUAGE IS THE ART OF SEEING
WHAT OTHERS ARE THINKING*